Making a I

John Boakes

Smith
Settle

First published in 2001 by
Smith Settle Ltd
Ilkley Road
Otley
West Yorkshire
LS21 3JP

ISBN 1 85825 114 1

British Library Cataloguing-in-Publication data:
A catalogue record for this book is available from the British Library.

Set in Monotype Plantin

Designed, printed and bound by
SMITH SETTLE
Ilkley Road, Otley, West Yorkshire LS21 3JP

Introduction

Containers and barrels made from wood have been produced in great numbers since Egyptian times. In the past, brewery companies in particular have employed *coopers* or barrel-makers in large numbers to make barrels for their beers. In some of the larger companies there were more than 600 or 700 coopers employed at any one time. Unfortunately, though, with the introduction of metal and even plastic barrels for the transportation of beer in the 1950s and 1960s, fewer wooden barrels were needed, and this in time led to the subsequent laying-off in large numbers of highly skilled coopers. This meant that these craftsmen had to look for work elsewhere. Some chose to turn to carpentry, whilst others turned to dry coopering (see page 4), and a few just altered the size and shape of the barrels they made, and started to produce 'dolly tubs', water barrels and stable buckets. In a few cases, if the coopers lived by the sea, they sometimes chose to make fish barrels, and as a sideline even tried their hand at smoking fish as well. To provide fuel for these smoke houses, they used the sawdust obtained from the other woodworking jobs that they did.

In time, the numbers working for themselves in various other occupations increased. This had the knock-on effect of removing the need for taking on apprentices, and the knowledge of the complex procedures of coopering was gradually lost. This later led to the dying out of the trade for a short while. Luckily, in recent years, with the new-found popularity of real ale in pubs, a few breweries decided that they still needed the skills of a cooper to repair the few old wooden barrels that they still had, as well as to make a few new ones as they were needed. When they tried to employ coopers for this work, they found that coopering was a 'dead trade', so the only thing that they could do was to bring back the last of their old coopers, who had long since retired, to train a group of new apprentices. Now coopering has started to become a living craft again, and today there are at least ten brewery coopers and apprentices employed full time throughout the country.

The art of making barrels is divided into two. Firstly, there is *wet cooperage*: this deals with barrels or tubs made for use in the dairy, stable, brewery or distillery, in fact any situation where liquids are involved. Secondly there is *dry cooperage*, the less skilled of the two, because these barrels do not have to be watertight. The shape of a 'dry' barrel is also slightly different, being more bulbous in outline as well as being bound with wooden hoops. Though rarely used today, these barrels, tubs or kegs were used for transporting goods or materials such as ceramics, flour, fish, potatoes and ironware. But this trade also decreased with the introduction of cardboard and the dreaded shrink-proof plastic of today.

Barrel-making has altered little over the centuries, and wet coopers still insert rushes between the joints of the *heads* or lids at both ends of the barrel to ensure that the barrel is watertight. This is because, when the barrel is filled with liquid, the absorbent pith of the rush swells up and ensures a watertight joint. This practice is called *chiming the flag*. The 'chime' refers to the length of a *stave* or segment of the barrel between the *croze* or groove at each end. This croze is used to secure the heads of the barrel into.

The staves are slightly bow-shaped, giving the final curved outline of the barrel. Coopers are very particular about the quality of the wood that they use when making a barrel, and will only use oak of the highest quality. This wood must be without any knots or blemishes, and is usually cut only from the wood at the base of the tree and for two stave-lengths along the trunk. In recent times, with fewer mature oak trees being cut down and the availability of English wood decreasing, it has been necessary to import quantities of roughly shaped staves cut from Russian or German oak.

Oak has not always been used for barrels. The old-time coopers thought that oak barrels tainted the taste of the beer, and for a short period they tried making barrels from many other varieties of wood. It has since been found, however, that there is little, if any, truth in this claim, and oak has always been used for the past 100 years or so in the making of barrels.

Once the staves have been shaped, the cooper checks to see how they fit together; this is called *setting up the barrel*. To hold the staves together in this early stage of manufacture, an ash hoop was used. When the barrel was finally finished, the wooden hoops were replaced with iron bands. In recent times these ash hoops have been replaced with iron ones.

At its height, coopering was a very well-paid occupation: in the 1920s a skilled cooper would be earning around £5 10s (£5.50) a week, nearly twice the average wage.

Once a barrel has been made, it is branded with the brewer's name and a number to keep a record of it in use. A barrel usually lasts for about fifty years. During that time it requires only a little maintenance, such as the changing of the iron hoops or the fitting of a new head.

Theakstons of Masham, North Yorkshire, still uses a large number of barrels for transporting its fine ales, and its cooper, Jonathan Manby, is featured in the latter part of this book, where he shows some of the techniques used in the making and maintaining of a barrel.

Bibliography

James Arnold, *The Shell Book of Country Crafts* (1968).
Herbert Edlin, *Woodland Craft of Britain* (1949 & 1973).
H E Fitzrandolph & M D Hay, *The Rural Crafts of England and Wales* (1926 & 1977).
J E Manners, *Country Crafts Today* (1974).
David Morgan Rees, *Yorkshire Craftsmen at Work* (1999).

Acknowledgements

The author would like to thank: Jonathan Manby of Theakstons Brewery, Masham, North Yorkshire; Nicola Mills of the Beamish Photographic Library for the use of the photographs on pages 8, 9, 10 & 46; and Caroline Benson of the Rural History Centre at Reading University for the photos on pages 26-7.

An old barrel stands on a *cooper's stool* awaiting repair.
One of the old metal bands has already been removed.

An engraving by John Miller showing a cooper at work in the early nineteenth century.

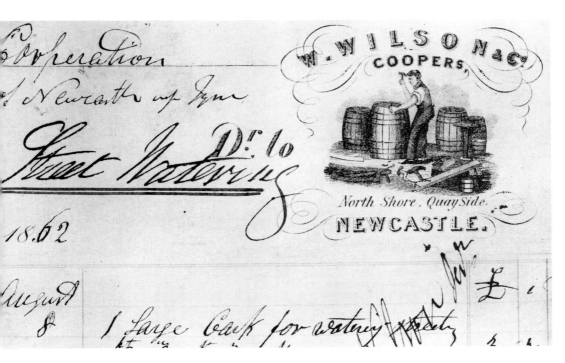

An 1862 letterhead from W Wilson & Co of Newcastle, showing a cooper fitting an iron hoop.

Former cooper Mr Arthur Hill proudly displaying some of his work some time around the 1940s.

Jonathan Manby in his workshop at Theakstons Brewery, Masham, North Yorkshire.

A roughly shaped stave, newly imported from Russia or Germany.

Shaping the stave with a *hallowing drawshave*.

The stave half finished

Two finished staves with the characteristic barrel shape.

An *end band* is made to the right size to fit the barrel being made.

(Left) The required number of staves is positioned in a *setting-up ring* and the end band is fitted in place; and *(right)* a smaller setting-up ring is then used to pull the staves into a barrel shape.

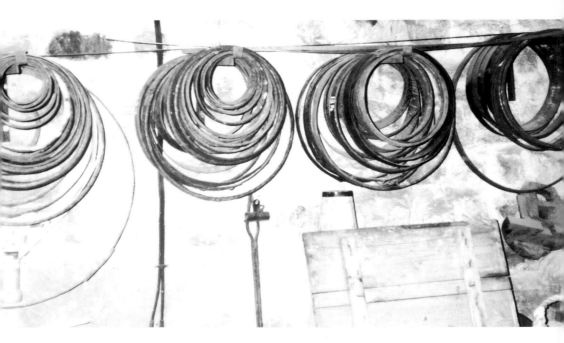

A selection of setting-up rings waiting to be used.

After the bands have been put on, a small brazier called a *cressie* is used to 'fire' the inside of the barrel to seal it and clear away any impurities received during manufacture.

The position of the *heads*, or the top and bottom, of the barrel are marked.

A *crow plane* is used to make the groove or *rebate* that will hold the head in position.

When the rebate is cut, a reed is placed in it to make sure that the head will be watertight.

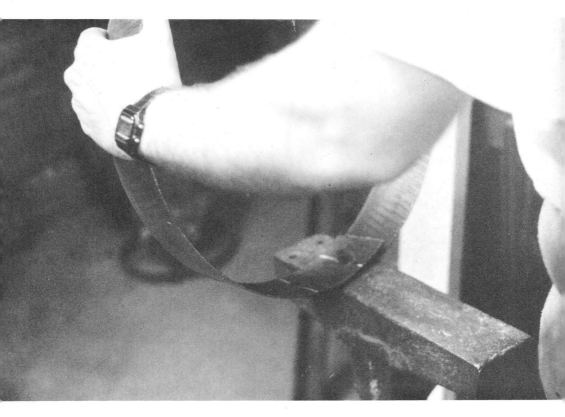

...howing how the bands are cold riveted together. Nowadays, the metal for the bands is bought in already made to the correct width.

The head is then made. You can see an old head with the shaped edge that fits into the rebate

Each joint of the head is smoothed with a cooper's *side axe*.

An old-time cooper making a dry barrel: *(facing page left)* using a *drawshave* to shape the edge of the head; *(facing page right)* *compassing* the top; *(left)* securing the head.

Jonathan drills holes in to each section of the head and fits wooden dowels.

Lengths of imported rush are used between the joints to ensure that the head is watertight.

How the lengths of rush are fitted around the dowels.

Once Jonathan has finished and fitted the heads, the barrel is nearly complete.

Finally, the two end bands are secured into position with the *flogger*. A flogger is a length of iron bar that the cooper has shaped at one end to make a handle. The bulk of a cooper's tools are either made by him or passed down to him by retiring coopers.

Before a barrel is used, it must have the name of the brewery and its own number stamped on it. This number records when it was made and any subsequent repairs throughout its life at the brewery.

Repairing the stock of old barrels is another of Jonathan's jobs.

Here Jonathan can be seen repairing an old barrel. He has removed the old head and is cleaning up the inside joints of the barrel with a *roundshave*.

A drawshave is used to even up the outside edges of the staves.

Once the edges are finished, the iron band is next to be replaced.

The four old bands of a barrel lie discarded on the floor. Notice the joints of each band with its rivet.

(Left) The new band is marked off to the right length; *(below)* and the overlap of the new band is measured and marked off to the right length.

(Left) Once the new band is made, it is only part-fitted into position before the middle bands are done. *(Right)* When the middle bands have been fitted, the head band is then hammered into position with the flogger.

newly repaired barrel.

(Above) The *bung auger* is used to make the holes in a barrel to allow filling.

(Top right) A selection of *downright planes* lies on the work bench.

(Right) The T-shaped cooper's anvil, or *bick iron*.

Old barrels waiting to be repaired. One of the two large barrels at the back is for whisky, the other for port.

A wooden bucket made by Jonathan for the Ryedale Folk Museum, North Yorkshire.

Clive Hollis
of Theakstons
Brewery tighten—
ing up the *bush*
or cap on the
millionth barrel
of its Old Peculier
Ale.

An old poster by Gilroy showing the *trussing-in* ceremony of a cooper after finishing his apprenticeship.

In June 1999, Jonathan Manby was trussed in as a fully qualified cooper af⟨⟩ his four-year apprenticed training — the last person to qualify in the twenti⟨⟩ century — and is now one of only eight working coopers left in the count⟨⟩